BEGINNINGS

HUMANS

ORIGINS AND EVOLUTION

Evolution of the Universe

4.5 billion years ago the oceans and first landmasses form. 9

1 million years after the Big Bang, hydrogen atoms form. 5

10-20 billion years ago, in less than a second, four things happen.

1. The Big Bang
2. Inflation
3. The beginning of the four forces
4. The first atomic nuclei form

1 billion years after the Big Bang, galaxies begin to form. 6

8 4.6 billion years ago
   the Earth's crust forms.

7 5 billion years ago
   the planet Earth forms.

11 2.5 billion years ago
    the atmosphere forms.

10 3 billion years ago
    bacteria appear—
    life begins.

BEGINNINGS

Humans

ORIGINS AND EVOLUTION

by
Fiorenzo Facchini

English Translation by Rocco Serini

Belitha Press

© Copyright 1993, Editoriale Jaca Book spa, Milan

First published in the United Kingdom in 1994 by

Belitha Press
31 Newington Green
London N16 9PU

English translation © 1994 by Steck-Vaughn Company

Cataloguing in print data available from the British Library

ISBN 1 85561 379 4

Graphics and Layout: The Graphics Department of Jaca Book
Special thanks to the Museum of Natural History of Milan
Illustrations: Giorgio Bacchin p. 9 (1), p. 12-13, p. 14 (4), step, p. 17 (2), p. 18 (2), p. 19 (3), p. 22-23, p. 24 (3), p.26 (1), p. 28 (2), p. 31 (3), p. 34 (1);
Severino Baraldi p. 21 (1);
Remo Berselli p. 17 (4), p. 24 (1), p. 25 (4), p. 29 (3);
Giacinto Gaudenzi p. 37 (5, 6);
Ezio Giglioli p. 15 (5, 6);
Antonio Molino p. 21 (2, 6), p. 27 (4), p. 31 (2), p. 33 (3), p. 36 (1, 2), p. 37 (4), p. 39 (1, 3), p. 40 (1), p. 41 (4, 5);
Lorenzo Orlandi p. 8-9 (2, 3, 4), p. 14-15 (2, 3), p. 20-21 (3, 4)

Printed and bound in the United States

Contents

The word billion is used throughout this book to mean one thousand million or 1 000 000 000.

Humans on Earth

When we look at the world around us, it is hard to imagine it being any different. One of the hardest parts is to imagine a world without people. But there were no people for most of the Earth's history. Humans **evolved** only about two million years ago. This may sound like a long time, but if you consider the age of the Earth, it's only a moment in time.

One minute before midnight

To help you understand how two million years can be only a moment, think of the Earth's age as a 24-hour day. If all of the Earth's life of 4.6 billion years is thought of as one day, humans would not appear until one minute before midnight.

1 *A prehistoric human holds a clock-shaped rock to show important events in the Earth's history in our 24-hour day.*
2 *About two hours before midnight it was the end of the Silurian Period, about 400 million years ago. The land was marshy and simple plants were beginning to evolve.*
3 *About one and a half hours before midnight it was the Carboniferous Period, 345 to 280 million years ago. The Earth's landmasses were covered with forests in which were giant ferns. Amphibians and insects were common and reptiles were just beginning to appear.*
4 *In the last hour before midnight, it was the Permian Period, 250 million years ago. Most of the marshy areas had dried up and reptiles, especially the dinosaurs, ruled the land. The dinosaur in the picture is Edaphosauria.*
5 *In the last half hour of the day, 70 million years ago, the first primate, Purgatorius, evolved.*
6 *Ancestors of modern humans (Homo habilis) appeared in the last minute of the day, only two million years ago.*

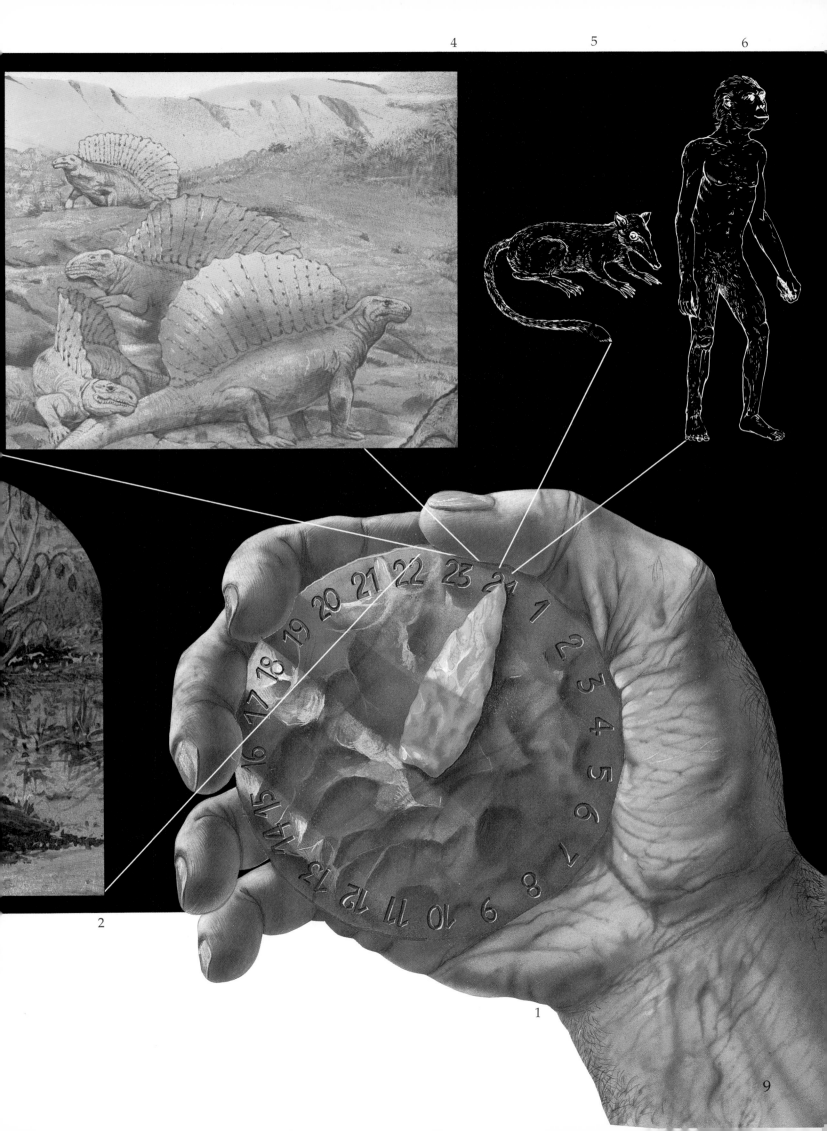

Human fossils

How can we find out about our past? Some of the most reliable information comes from **fossils**. Fossils are the remains of dead animals and plants, which have been preserved over many years. The most common remains of animals are bones, teeth and shells. But careful digging may also reveal traces of animals, such as their footprints. Traces of humans also include tools that they made or the remains of simple huts.

Learning from fossils

In the past hundred years, various human fossils have been found. These fossils are evidence of how human **species** have **evolved**, or changed over millions of years. Some early fossil bones and teeth are very similar to those of modern humans. Other fossils show species related to humans as well as to other **primates**. Fossil traces of early humans can tell us about their culture. Carefully carved stones, for example, give us information about how our human ancestors lived millions of years ago.

Evidence of evolution

Human fossils give important evidence in support of the idea of human evolution. There are people who have doubts about whether humans really did evolve from other animals. But there is evidence to show that the animals and plants we know today evolved from other forms of living things. Human and prehuman fossils also show how species of humans gradually evolved over two million years.

1 *This is a chopper, a simple stone tool, found at a site in Ethiopia, along with the fossil bones of one of the first types of human.*
2 *These traces are fossil footprints discovered in Laetoli, Tanzania. They show that ancestors of modern humans walked on this part of the Earth over three million years ago.*
3 *These fossils are from an important archaeological site in Hadar, Ethiopia. At the back of the table are skulls of chimpanzees that are being used for comparison. In the foreground are the bones of Australopithecus afarensis, an ancestor of modern humans.*

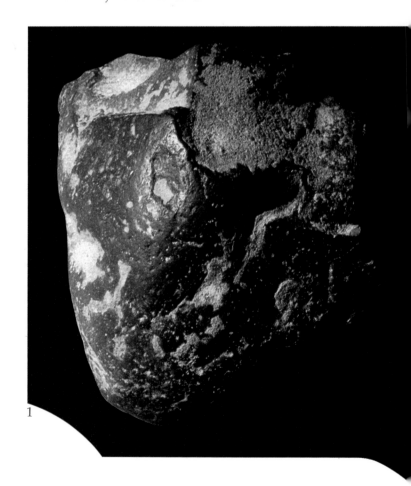

1

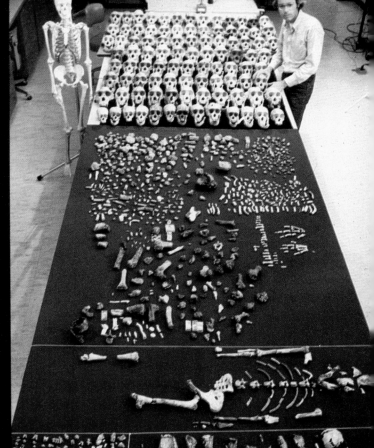

4 *This is the site in Ethiopia where remains of Homo erectus, one ancestor of modern humans, was found.*

5 *These stone tools were found at a site in Ethiopia where Homo habilis, another ancestor of modern humans, once lived.*

Evolution of humans

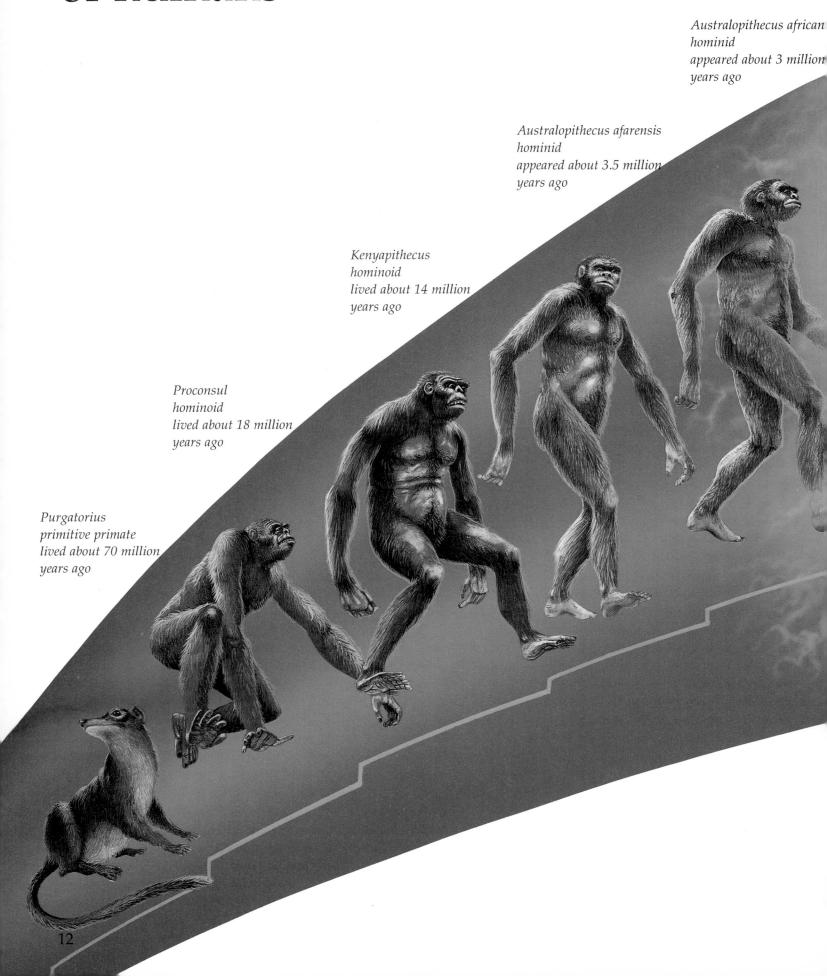

Australopithecus african
hominid
appeared about 3 million
years ago

Australopithecus afarensis
hominid
appeared about 3.5 million
years ago

Kenyapithecus
hominoid
lived about 14 million
years ago

Proconsul
hominoid
lived about 18 million
years ago

Purgatorius
primitive primate
lived about 70 million
years ago

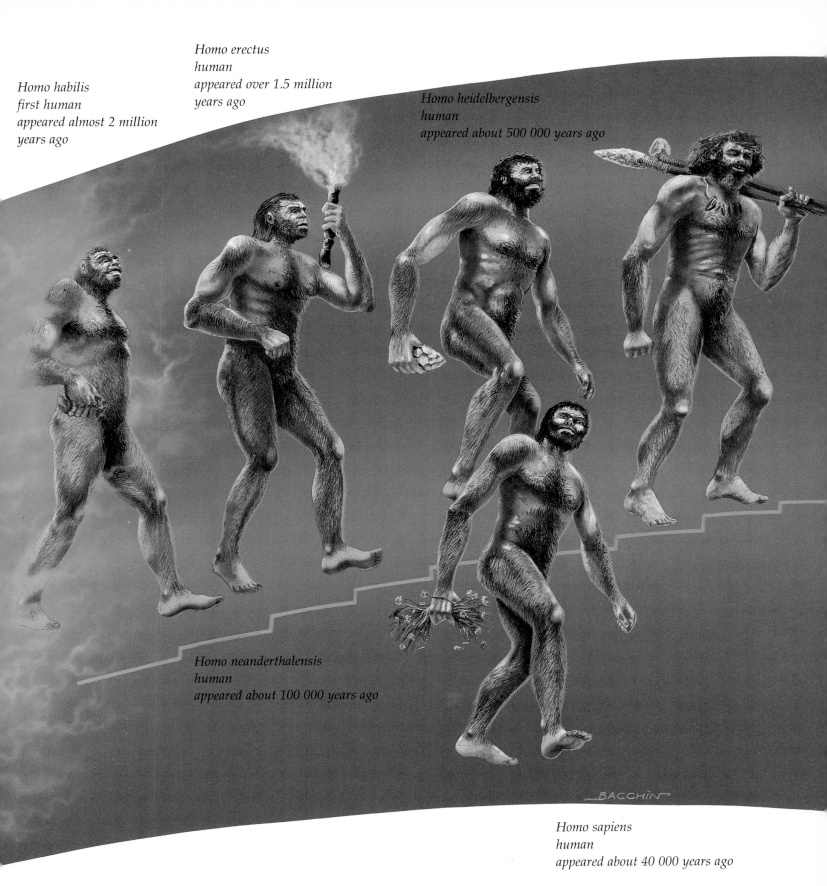

Homo habilis
first human
appeared almost 2 million
years ago

Homo erectus
human
appeared over 1.5 million
years ago

Homo heidelbergensis
human
appeared about 500 000 years ago

Homo neanderthalensis
human
appeared about 100 000 years ago

BACCHIN

Homo sapiens
human
appeared about 40 000 years ago

The first primates

Primate: Purgatorius   *Hominoid: Proconsul*   *Hominoid: Kenyapithec*

The first **mammals** appeared on Earth over 200 million years ago. They were small, fur-covered animals that hid in the forests. Their fur helped them to keep their body heat and allowed them to be active at night while the dinosaurs slept.

Primates belong to the order of mammals which includes humans. The first ones evolved about 65 million years ago. These primates were like other mammals of the time in that they were small – about the size of a mouse – and furry. They probably ate insects.

Five toes

Like other mammals, primates had five toes on each foot. The feet of most mammals evolved over time into specially **adapted** paws or hoofs. Primates kept the five digits. Having a thumb opposite four fingers allows them to grasp objects. This makes the hands of primates very useful. The thumb has padded surfaces that can press against the padded surfaces of other fingers.

Early fossils

Prosimians, which means 'before the apes', are simpler types of primates. The earliest prosimians looked like rodents. One of the earliest prosimian fossils, named *Purgatorius*, was found in Montana, in the United States. This was part of a large continent made up of North America and Europe 65 million years ago. Primates may have evolved in the coniferous forests of this huge continent.

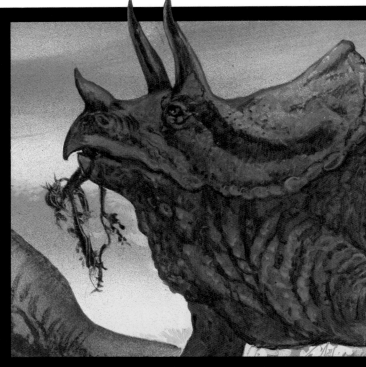

3

1 A fossil fragment of a jaw bone of Purgatorius. Notice the sharp teeth. These primates ate insects and fruits.
2 Purgatorius looked like a rat and had 44 teeth.
3 Triceratops was one of the dinosaurs that ruled the Earth when mammals were starting to evolve.
4 The large continent where primates may have evolved was separated from Africa, Asia and South America.

1

2 →

Hominid:
Australopithecus afarensis

Hominid:
Australopithecus africanus

Homo habilis

Homo erectus

Homo heidelbergensis

Homo neanderthalensis

Homo sapiens

4

5

6

5 This modern prosimian is the Sifakas from Madagascar.

6 The tarsier is a living prosimian which is found throughout the Philippines and Malaysia.

The first hominoids

It is difficult for scientists to trace how the primates evolved. They know that primates first appeared in the combined European and North American continent. Fossils from later primates have been found in Africa and Asia. How were the findings linked?

Changes in the Earth's surface

The evolution of primates was affected by geological changes. During this period of tens of millions of years, the surface of the Earth was changing. Continents moved together and apart. Water levels in the ocean rose and fell, making possible land bridges between continents. But this is only part of the puzzle.

Lack of fossil evidence

Our knowledge of primate evolution is based on fossil finds. Fossils occur only where mud, soil or sand bury and preserve parts of a skeleton. Sometimes these parts are tiny pieces of bone, and reconstructing the animal is very difficult. But that is better than not finding any fossils at all. There are areas where animals lived and died without leaving a trace. Their skeletons turned to dust or were buried under piles of rock.

The hominoid Proconsul

One important fossil species found in the eastern part of Africa is a primate species named **Proconsul**. It lived about 18 million years ago. *Proconsul* was not a prosimian. It was a **hominoid**, or higher primate, sharing traits with modern apes and humans.

Some of its bones look like those of a monkey. But this animal had a much larger brain than modern monkeys do. Although the *Proconsul* species did not swing through the trees, they did live in trees. *Proconsul* is thought to be an ancestor of all modern apes and humans.

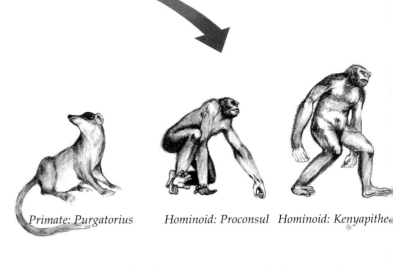

Primate: Purgatorius   Hominoid: Proconsul   Hominoid: Kenyapithe

1, 2, 3 *These maps show how landmasses might have moved. The landmasses during the Eocene Epoch from about 53 to 36 million years ago are shown in 1. North America and Europe have separated, and Asia has merged with Europe. A land bridge south of modern-day Spain connects Europe and Africa. Europe and Africa have separated in 2. A different land bridge (shown in 3) may have later reconnected Africa with the Eurasian continent during the Miocene Epoch.*

4 *A reconstruction of Proconsul shows that this primate looked like many modern primates and was very different from its ancestor, Purgatorius.*

5 *This skull of Proconsul was found by Mary Leakey in Kenya, in East Africa.*

6 *A modern gorilla is probably only one of the species which have descended from Proconsul. This one, living in a zoo, was lonely until it was given a kitten as a pet.*

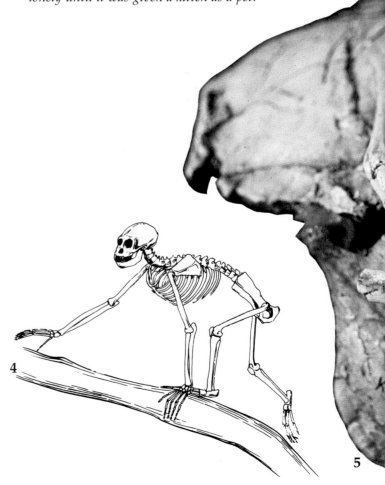

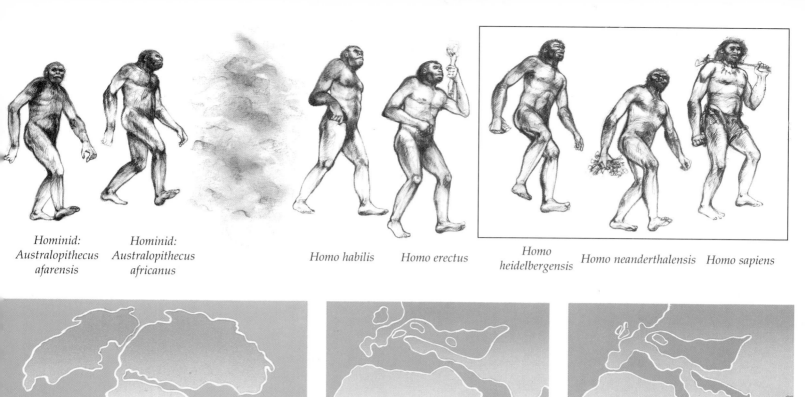

Hominid:
Australopithecus afarensis

Hominid:
Australopithecus africanus

Homo habilis

Homo erectus

Homo heidelbergensis

Homo neanderthalensis

Homo sapiens

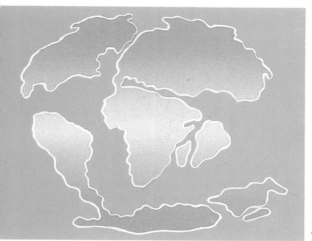

1

2

3

4

An East-African hominoid

Over a period of several million years, some hominoids evolved. They became more similar to modern humans and less like modern monkeys. These later hominoids were better adapted to living in open woodlands than in dense forests.

Primate: Purgatorius   Hominoid: Proconsul   Hominoid: Kenyapith...

Changes in the later hominoids

Kenyapithecus, a fossil hominoid species, lived about 14 million years ago in East Africa. This homonoid had long, sturdy arms and legs. It could climb trees as well as walk around in open areas. Its head was flatter than that of the early hominoids and less pointed or snoutlike, with a larger, stronger jaw. A thick layer of enamel covered its teeth. The stronger jaw and teeth meant that *Kenyapithecus* and other later hominoids could eat the many different foods available in the woodlands.

By looking at fossils of later hominoids, scientists can tell that their final set of teeth took a long time to grow. This shows that the hominoid took a long time to mature. Like humans, the young were cared for over a long period of time.

1

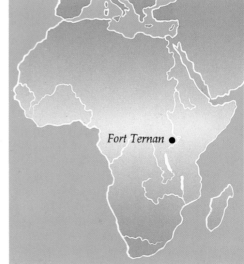

2

1 *Louis Leakey, pictured here, and his wife Mary, found many African fossils.*
2 *Louis Leakey found Kenyapithecus in Fort Ternan, Kenya. The fossil was named after the country where it was found.*
3 *This is an artist's impression of how Kenyapithecus lived. This hominoid was adapted to both the moist environment of the forest and dry, open grassland.*
4 *In this reconstruction of a skull of Kenyapithecus, you can see the strong, thick jaw. Notice also how the face is less pointed or snoutlike.*
5 *A block of basalt and some chipped bones were found with Kenyapithecus. This hominoid may have used tools.*

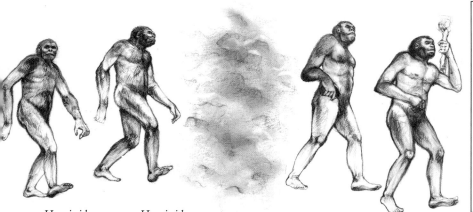

Hominid:
Australopithecus
afarensis

Hominid:
Australopithecus
africanus

Homo habilis

Homo erectus

Homo
heidelbergensis

Homo neanderthalensis

Homo sapiens

3

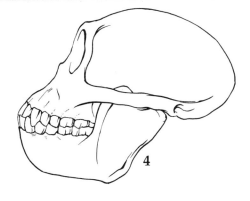

4

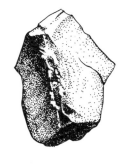

5

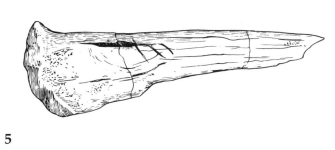

The pace of evolution

We know that evolution does not always occur at a slow and steady pace. There is evidence that whole species can disappear in a relatively short period of time. One of the best known disappearances or **extinctions** was that of the dinosaurs. The reason for this extinction is not clear. It may have been caused by dust after a massive meteorite collided with the Earth; or it may have been caused by the beginning of a new Ice Age.

The Rift Valley forms

During the Miocene Age, about 20 million years ago, there were changes in the structure of the African continent. The plates that form the Earth's crust moved, causing a gigantic split along the length of the African continent. Volcanoes spewed lava and ash, mountains rose, valleys formed and huge lakes filled.

The newly formed Rift Valley divided Africa into two parts. Rains blowing in from the Atlantic kept the area to the west of the valley well-watered. The land stayed much as it was, filled with rain forests and lush plant life. But the rains did not pass to the eastern part because of the mountains of the Rift Valley. So here in the east the land was dry. Instead of forests, there were large open grasslands.

Homonids appear

As the land and plants in the eastern part of Africa changed, some animals adapted to their new environment, while others became extinct. Hominoids that had lived successfully in the forests and woodlands were not adapted to this new environment.

Fossils indicate that **hominids** appeared in this new environment. Hominids are the group of primates that include humans and their fossil relatives.

These primates were humanlike. They walked on two feet. Although they were not fast runners, they probably were faster than the knuckle-walking great apes. Their upright posture would have been an advantage for seeing prey or danger in the distance. Hominid fossils show that their brains grew larger than those of other hominoids.

1 *This map of Africa shows how the climate affects plant and animal life in different regions. The dense rain forests of the west support a few types of hominoids, including chimpanzees and gorillas. The savannahs are drier areas with few trees. Grasslands, or prairies, are even drier than savannahs. Hominids evolved in the grasslands and savannahs east of the Rift Valley.*
2 *This shows how the Rift Valley extends from the Red Sea to the south of Africa.*
3, 4 *Chimpanzees (3) and gorillas (4) evolved from common hominoid ancestors.*
5 *On the left is a gorilla. It can stand and even walk upright, but its body is not adapted to walking on two legs. On the right, the human body is straighter, more vertical and balanced above the legs. This allows humans to walk and run easily. This straightening has drawbacks for humans. The spine curves so that the head is directly above the pelvis, and this often causes backache.*
6 *This set of footprints, made by two individuals in soft, volcanic ash, 3.5 million years ago, is exciting evidence that hominids walked upright.*

3

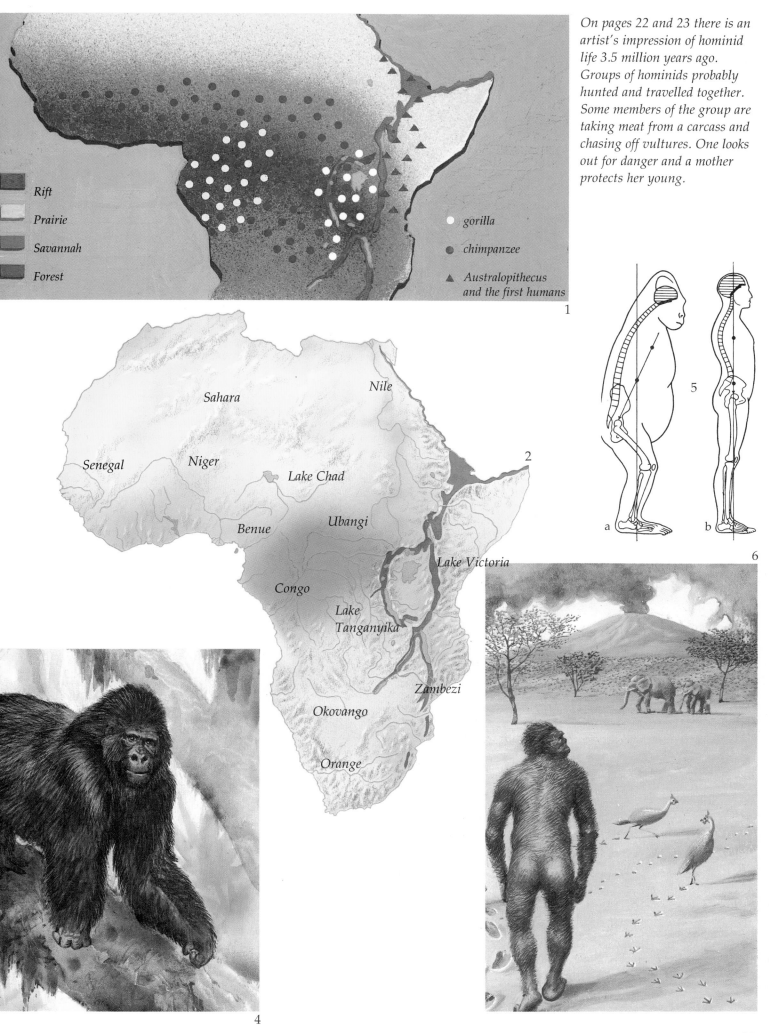

On pages 22 and 23 there is an artist's impression of hominid life 3.5 million years ago. Groups of hominids probably hunted and travelled together. Some members of the group are taking meat from a carcass and chasing off vultures. One looks out for danger and a mother protects her young.

Rift
Prairie
Savannah
Forest

○ gorilla
● chimpanzee
▲ Australopithecus and the first humans

1

Sahara

Nile

Senegal

Niger

Lake Chad

Benue

Ubangi

Lake Victoria

Congo

Lake Tanganyika

Zambezi

Okovango

Orange

2

a   b

5

6

4

A fossil called Lucy

Sometimes lucky fossil finds can give us a vivid glimpse of the past. One such find was in northern Ethiopia where a fossil called Lucy was discovered in 1981.

Primate: Purgatorius   Hominoid: Proconsul   Hominoid: Kenyapithe

Lucy

Lucy is a collection of bones all from the same person who lived about 3.2 million years ago. It is unusual to find so much of one skeleton. Putting the collection of bones together, scientists have calculated that this individual was probably female and stood about 60 centimetres tall. Although this would be the size of a child today, Lucy may have been an adult. Lucy had relatively long arms, which showed that the ancestors of her species had swung from branch to branch through dense forests.

Lucy's brain was smaller than that of a modern human. Compared with apes, her brain was large. Her bones indicate that she walked upright on two legs. For this reason, Lucy is classified as a hominid, a species related to humans. This stage in hominid evolution is a species called ***Australopithecus afarensis.***

Other fossil finds

In 1992, scientists discovered a skull very close to the place where Lucy was found. The skull was in hundreds of pieces. This fossil is another exciting piece of evidence in the study of our earliest ancestors.

Fossils of *Australopithecus afarensis* have also been found in Tanzania. These bones are several hundred thousand years older than Lucy. It was in Tanzania that the fossil footprints on page 21 were made in the soft volcanic ash. The footprints provide further evidence that these hominids walked upright.

1 *Notice the large brow ridges and protruding jaw in this skull of Australopithecus afarensis.*
2 *This may be the way Australopithecus afarensis looked. Scientists cannot be certain whether they were fur-covered because fossils cannot show this, but most scientists think that they had hairier bodies than modern humans.*
3 *Lucy was found in Hadar, Ethiopia. Other Australopithecus afarensis fossils were found in Laetoli in Tanzania.*

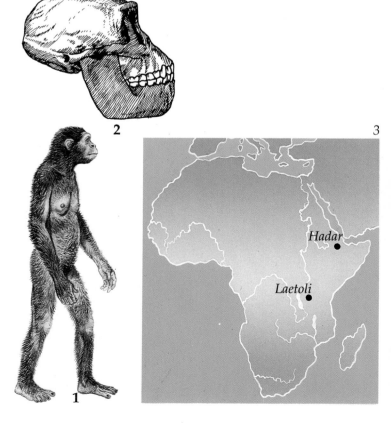

Hominid: Australopithecus afarensis *Hominid: Australopithecus africanus* *Homo habilis* *Homo erectus* *Homo heidelbergensis* *Homo neanderthalensis* *Homo sapiens*

4

4 *Australopithecus afarensis might have lived together in small groups. This reconstruction shows males going off to hunt, leaving the young with a female.*

5 *The skeleton of Lucy.*

5

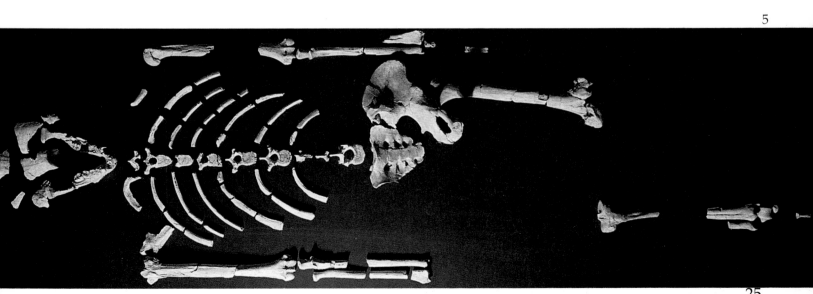

More African discoveries

Tracing our human origins is difficult because fossils usually consist of just a few bones. Educated guesses have to be made using only a part of a skull or a handful of teeth. The real problem is that most of the hominids died without leaving any trace.

Fossil find at Taung

Just part of a skull was enough to identify **Australopithecus africanus**. A scientist in South Africa, called Raymond Dart, was given a box of fossils which had been found in a mine at Taung, a remote spot in southern Africa.

The bones were from the face and jaw of a young child. There was also a cast of the brain. This had been formed when limestone and water collected inside the skull. This brain was small compared with that of a modern human, but it was larger than the brain of *Australopithecus afarensis*.

New species of hominid

Other fossil finds confirmed that this was a newly discovered species of hominid. Like *Australopithecus afarensis* this species still had well-developed and large arms, well-suited for climbing trees. Both were well-adapted to walking on two feet. Slight differences between the fossils suggest that *Australopithecus africanus* evolved from *Australopithecus afarensis*, making it a step closer to modern humans.

Other fossil finds

Fossils found in South Africa had flat faces, as well as very large jaws and molars that would help them chew plant parts. These hominids are usually called *Australopithecus robustus*.

Mary and Louis Leakey discovered the remains of a related species in Eastern Africa. This species is named *Australopithecus boisei*. It is even more robust, or hefty, than *Australopithecus robustus*.

Primate: Purgatorius   *Hominoid: Proconsul*   *Hominoid: Kenyapith*

1 *The first Australopithecus africanus fossils were found in a mine at Taung, South Africa. Australopithecus boisei was found in Olduvai Gorge in Eastern Africa.*
2 *This is a reconstruction of the young Australopithecus africanus based on the skull found in Taung.*
3 *This is what the skull found in Taung looked like.*
4 *This artist's impression shows an Australopithecus group. They probably travelled in groups for safety and for the protection of their young. Although they were not able to hunt large animals, they may have been able to catch small animals. Their main diet was plants and scavenged animal meat.*
5 *Reconstruction of Australopithecus boisei.*

1

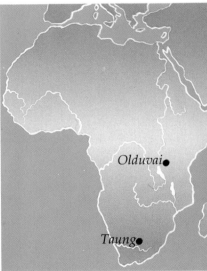

Olduvai

Taung

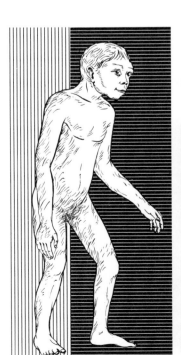

2   3

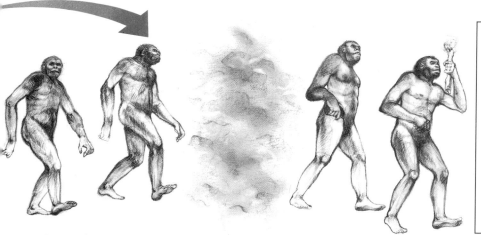

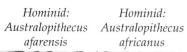 *Hominid:
Australopithecus
afarensis*

*Hominid:
Australopithecus
africanus*

Homo habilis

Homo erectus

*Homo
heidelbergensis*

Homo neanderthalensis

Homo sapiens

4

5

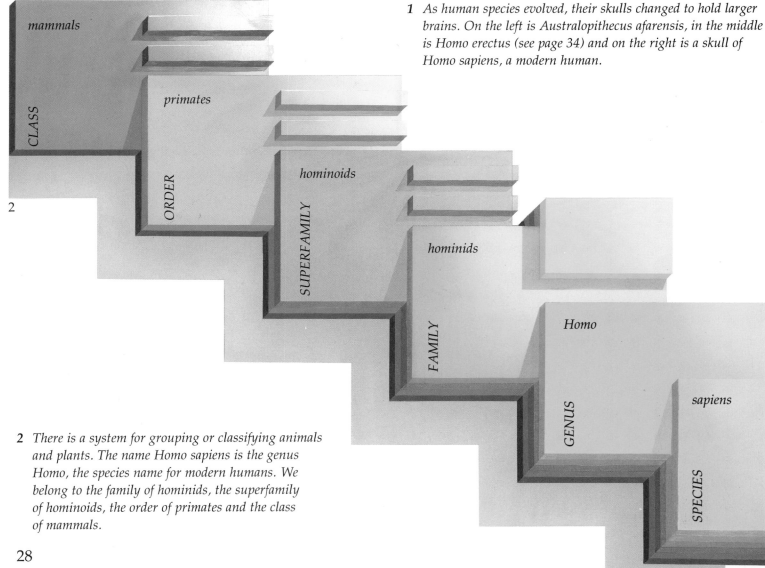

1 As human species evolved, their skulls changed to hold larger brains. On the left is Australopithecus afarensis, in the middle is Homo erectus (see page 34) and on the right is a skull of Homo sapiens, a modern human.

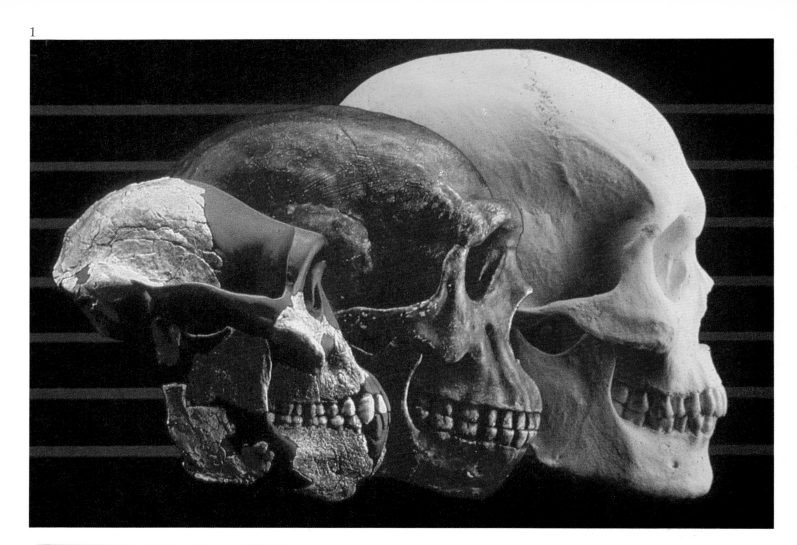

mammals

CLASS

primates

ORDER

hominoids

SUPERFAMILY

hominids

FAMILY

Homo

GENUS

sapiens

SPECIES

2 There is a system for grouping or classifying animals and plants. The name Homo sapiens is the genus Homo, the species name for modern humans. We belong to the family of hominids, the superfamily of hominoids, the order of primates and the class of mammals.

Hominids to humans

Human evolution is like all other types of animal evolution – as the environment changed, so human species adapted to the new conditions. It is important to remember that this change is still going on, that we are still evolving. Of course, we cannot see how humans are evolving now. It is a process which takes millions of years.

Because evolution is about gradual change, it is hard to find an exact time when a certain primate became a human. But it is possible to find fossils of primate species whose descendants evolved into modern humans.

Walking upright and having two feet

These two features are important in human evolution. We know that Australopithecus had two feet and could walk upright. Walking on two legs is faster than the knuckle-walk of some other primates. Whatever the reasons for developing the upright walk, it leaves the hands free for other things. They could be used to carry things, and eventually to form tools or create art.

Handy man

A fossil species that can be viewed as a distinct step in human evolution is *Homo habilis* (see page 30). This species used and made tools. Its brain was larger than that of some other hominoid species.

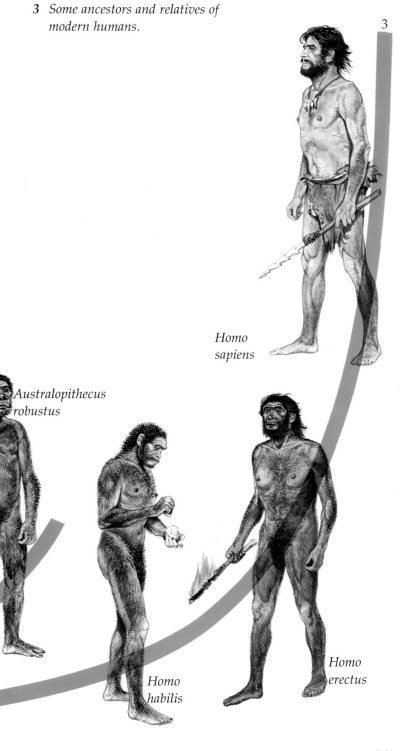

3 *Some ancestors and relatives of modern humans.*

Homo sapiens

Australopithecus robustus

Australopithecus africanus

Homo habilis

Homo erectus

29

Using tools

Collections of stone tools were found with the fossils of hominids that came after *Australopithecus africanus*. These tools were very similar in shape and form. The stones seem to have been specially chosen and then shaped into tools. This shows that their users

  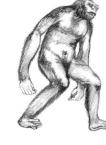

Primate: Purgatorius *Hominoid: Proconsul* *Hominoid: Kenyapithe*

1 *This photograph of the area near Hadar in Ethiopia shows the type of landscape where hominids evolved. As the land became drier, forests died out and were replaced by savannahs and grasslands.*

2 *This artist's impression shows a group of Homo habilis. Groups probably roamed the countryside and did not build shelters.*

were planning what they were going to do with the tools. This level of thought is considered unique to humans. For this reason, this tool-making hominid, which lived from about 2 to 1.5 million years ago, is named *Homo habilis*, also known as 'handy man'.

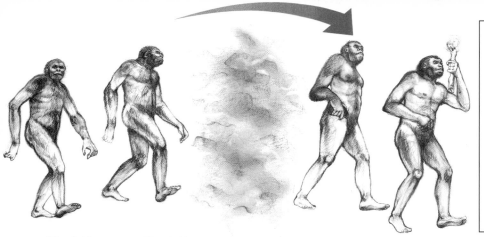

Hominid: Australopithecus afarensis

Hominid: Australopithecus africanus

Homo habilis

Homo erectus

Homo heidelbergensis

Homo neanderthalensis

Homo sapiens

2

Omo

Koobi Fora

Olduvai

Sterkfontein

3

3 Homo habilis fossils have been found in Omo, Ethiopia; in Koobi Fora, Kenya; in Olduvai Gorge, Tanzania; and in Sterkfontein, South Africa.

Human or not?

Homo habilis was physically very much like Australopithecus. Both were short and had similar skeletons. Although *Homo habilis* had a larger brain, it had more in common with Australopithecus than with modern humans. It may be a relative, not a direct ancestor, of modern humans.

31

What is human?

What is it that makes humans different from other animals? One of many possible answers is that humans have culture. Culture can be defined as things such as ideas, skills, customs, that are taught by one generation to the next.

1 Fossils of both Homo habilis and Homo erectus have been found in this area around the Awash River, Melka Kunture, in Ethiopia.

But if you are looking at bits of bone, how can you identify any group of beings as having or not having culture?

Evidence of culture

The scientists who examine homonoid fossils look for some kind of evidence of culture. Fossils cannot tell us about a language which is only spoken or signed, about customs or beliefs. They cannot even tell us if the beings made things out of wood, because wood disintegrates over time.

What does remain are tools made of stone, bone, antler or metal. Stone tools did not disintegrate, and they required time and effort to make. In order to tell whether a piece of chipped rock was a tool or merely a broken rock, archaeologists try to recreate the tools and to use them. They can match the wear marks on the tools and find out how the tools might have been used to dig, cut or crush.

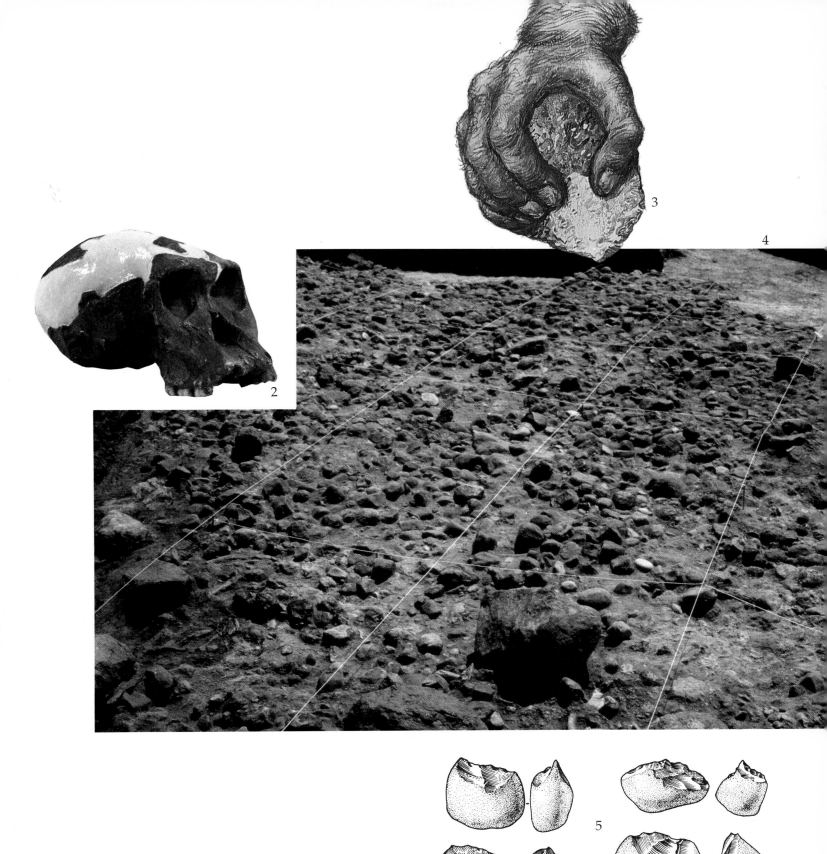

2 *This skull of Homo habilis was found at Koobi Fora, Kenya.*
3 *This is a recreation of a chopper, a simple stone tool which could be used for several purposes, including digging.*
4 *This is an archaeological excavation site at Melka Kunture. Strings mark off different areas so that the location of any find can be noted accurately. The ground is paved with stones, stone tools and animal bones.*
5 *Types of simple stone tools found at Olduvai Gorge in Tanzania. A stone tool could be given sharp edges by striking it against the side of another stone.*

Java Man

Charles Darwin published his famous book about evolution, *On the Origin of Species*, in 1859. Not long afterwards a young Dutch scientist called Eugene Dubois went to south-east Asia to look for remains of human ancestors. He was surprisingly lucky. He discovered part of a skull and some other bits of bone from what is sometimes called Java Man.

Java Man

Unlike modern humans, this fossil had a thick skull that was flat on the top and had large, heavy brow ridges. Because its skull was so different, scientists at the time had trouble accepting this as a type of human.

Other parts of the skeleton were almost identical to those of modern humans. For one thing, Java Man walked upright. Because of this it was given the name ***Homo erectus***. This name suggests that it was the first species to walk upright. We know now, from later discoveries of Australopithecus fossils, that this was not the case. Scientists of 100 years ago could not know that hominids were walking around Africa long before the time of *Homo erectus*.

Turkana boy

Some African fossils are also classified as *Homo erectus*. Turkana Boy is the fossil of a child that lived about 1.6 million years ago. Like Java Man, this fossil had a modern posture, but its skull was similar to that of modern humans – relatively thin and rounded.

Some scientists classify Turkana Boy as a different species, ***Homo ergaster.*** They think this species evolved into two different lines: one leading to modern humans; the other line evolving into the heavy, flat-skulled *Homo erectus*.

Homo erectus lived from about 1 million to 300 000 years ago. Although this species was a relative of modern humans, it is probably not a direct ancestor.

Primate: Purgatorius   Hominoid: Proconsul   Hominoid: Kenyapithe

1 *Fossils of Homo erectus and its relatives have been found in a large band across Africa, Europe and Asia. The first fossils found came from Europe and Asia, which made scientists think that the species evolved in one of those places. More recently, both Homo erectus and Homo ergaster have been found in Africa, so both may have evolved there.*

2, 3 *Reconstruction and the skull of Homo heidelbergensis found in a cave of Arago in southern France (see page 38).*

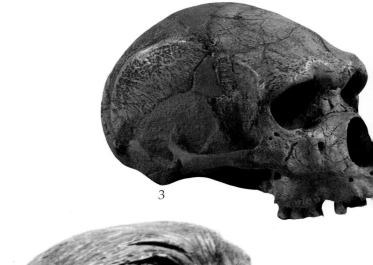

3

2

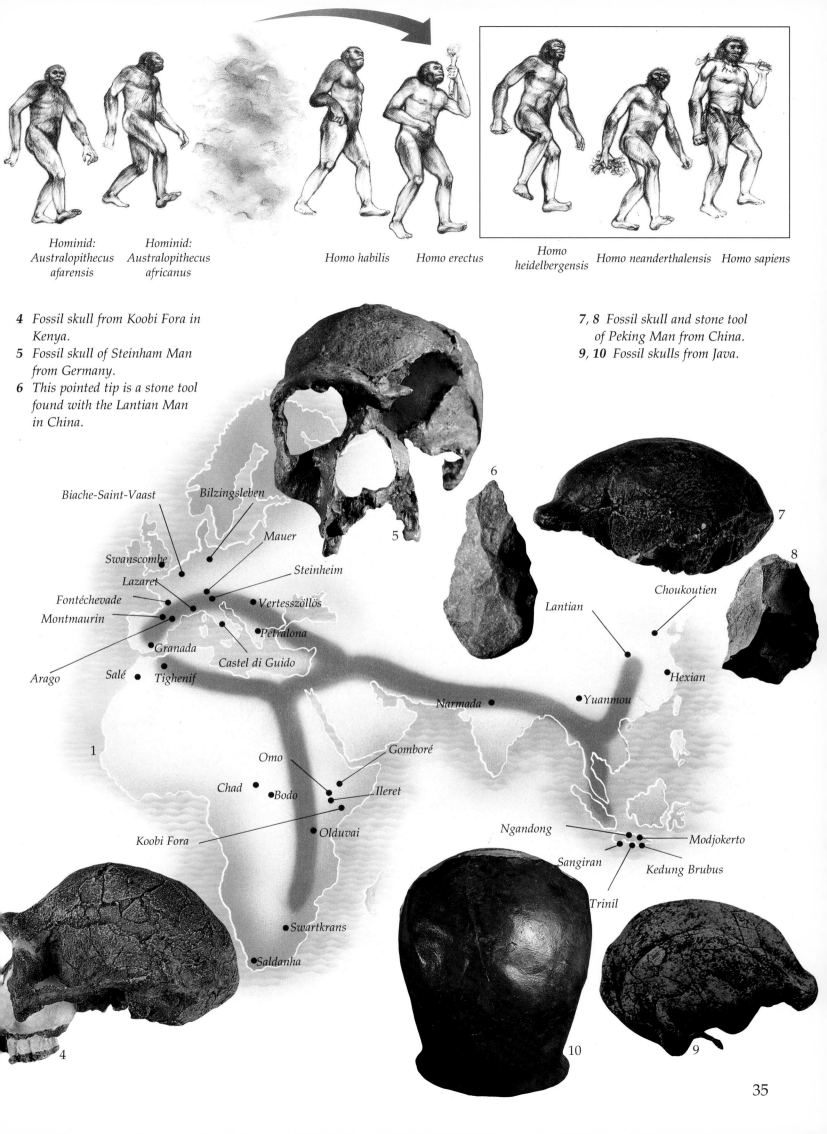

Hominid:
Australopithecus afarensis

Hominid:
Australopithecus africanus

Homo habilis

Homo erectus

Homo heidelbergensis

Homo neanderthalensis

Homo sapiens

4 Fossil skull from Koobi Fora in Kenya.
5 Fossil skull of Steinham Man from Germany.
6 This pointed tip is a stone tool found with the Lantian Man in China.

7, 8 Fossil skull and stone tool of Peking Man from China.
9, 10 Fossil skulls from Java.

Biache-Saint-Vaast
Bilzingsleben
Mauer
Swanscombe
Steinheim
Lazaret
Fontéchevade
Vertesszöllös
Montmaurin
Petralona
Granada
Castel di Guido
Arago
Salé
Tighenif

Lantian
Choukoutien
Hexian
Narmada
Yuanmou

Omo
Gomboré
Chad
Bodo
Ileret
Koobi Fora
Olduvai

Ngandong
Modjokerto
Sangiran
Kedung Brubus
Trinil

Swartkrans
Saldanha

Tools, fire and language

By 1.5 million years ago, stone tools were no longer just rocks with large chunks knocked off to form sharp edges. These simple tools were still made but new tools were appearing.

These new tools were worked over their entire surface, so that they had exact and predetermined shapes. Front, back and sides of a stone were chipped away to form pointed hand axes and broad-edged cleavers.

Use of tools

Probably these were used to dig up roots and to cut meat from carcasses left behind by other animals. It is likely that humans lived in small groups, eating mainly roots, plants and small animals. Living in groups gave them protection.

Use of fire

Fossils found in Africa at around the same time as the improved tools show some evidence of humans using fire. But much clearer evidence of humans using fire comes from later fossil finds in Europe.

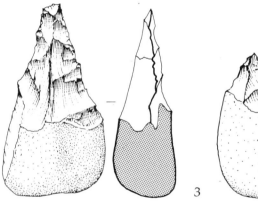
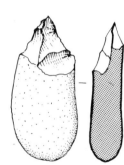

1 *An artist's impression of an early human camp. Layers of fossils show that different types of humans lived in the same places at various times.*
2 *Early humans probably first saw fires caused by lightning or by burning lava. In time, they learned to make their own fires by making sparks and setting light to dry grasses.*
3 *Stones which had been worked on all sides could form pointed tools for cutting and piercing.*
4 *This artist's impression shows early humans hunting elephants. Now scientists think that this did not happen, that early humans lived on plants and small animals and only took whatever meat was left on the carcasses of large animals.*

No one is certain how fire was used. At one time, archaeologists thought that fires may have been started to force large animals into traps. This was because bones of large animals were found along with human bones at some sites. But these finds can be misleading. Water often washed all the bones – human as well as animal – down from the spot where they actually died.

We can only guess how fire was used. It probably kept humans warm and safe from attack while they slept at night. It may have been used to cook food. It probably was a source of wonder. Like campfires today, a fire may have been a place to gather and communicate, or talk.

Language

Exactly how early humans communicated is even more of a mystery. All other species of animals, from bees to wolves, communicate with each other, so early humans must also have communicated. They needed to teach the young ones how to make tools and how to use them, as well as how to save and build a fire. But the language of very early humans may have been made up of signs and sounds, such as grunts, instead of words as we know them.

4

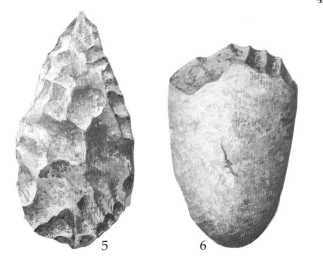

5, 6 Finely worked stone tools. The chopper on the right could be used to cut meat roughly from a carcass.

5 6

A new form of human

About 200 000 or 150 000 years ago, a new form of human evolved in Europe – the Neanderthals. This human is often thought of as shuffling, hulking and backward. But this may be because one of the first Neanderthal fossils found was the skeleton of an old person. He or she suffered from arthritis and, as a result, had a stooped posture and curved bones.

Later examples have a heavier skeleton, similar to our own, except for differences in the skull. The back of the skull extends in a large bump, and large brow ridges hang over the eyes. The jaws did not have a chin. They had very large brains which were even larger than those of modern humans.

A different species

Many scientists think that the Neanderthals were different enough from modern humans to be placed in a separate species – *Homo neanderthalensis.* This species is probably not a direct ancestor of *Homo sapiens*, or modern humans, but is instead a separate line of evolution. The ancestor of both these species is probably *Homo heidelbergensis*, whose remains have been found in both Europe and Africa.

We cannot be certain when *Homo neanderthalensis* lived. But probably starting about 90 000 years ago, during the last Ice Age, the Neanderthals spread all across Europe and Asia. They then died out about 35 000 years ago, when they were gradually replaced by *Homo sapiens*. Fossils of modern humans have been found in between layers of Neanderthal fossils. This shows that the two species lived not only at the same time but in the same places.

Primate: Purgatorius   *Hominoid: Proconsul*   *Hominoid: Kenyapithe*

1   *Fossil skull of Homo neanderthalensis found in La Chapelle aux Saintes in France.*
2   *Some Neanderthal fossils seem to have been buried intentionally. This shows that some Neanderthals had a form of religious belief. They may also have been able to speak, since being able to communicate and teach others is part of having religious beliefs.*
3   *Fossil skull of Homo sapiens.*

Earliest Homo sapiens fossils

The earliest *Homo sapiens* fossils from Europe are about 40 000 years old. These fossils are quite different from the Neanderthals. *Homo sapiens* are quite lightly built and have a different shaped head. The skull is lighter and more rounded at the back, with either small or no brow ridges. Unlike the Neanderthals, *Homo sapiens* have chins and small faces.

Fossils of forms between the Neanderthals and *Homo sapiens* have not been found in Europe. This shows that *Homo sapiens* probably did not evolve from the Neanderthal, and that it evolved in a different part of the world.

Fossils of modern humans about 100 000 years old have been found in Israel and Mediterranean Africa. Partial skeletons of modern and near-modern humans have been found in South Africa. These South African fossils may be as much as 120 000 years old, showing that Africa was a centre of important developments in the evolution of modern humans.

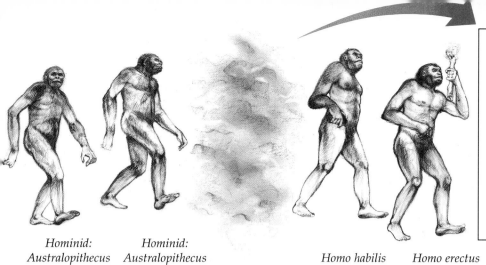

Hominid:
Australopithecus
afarensis

Hominid:
Australopithecus
africanus

Homo habilis

Homo erectus

Homo
heidelbergensis

Homo neanderthalensis

Homo sapiens

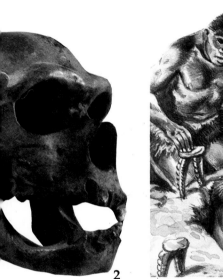

2

3

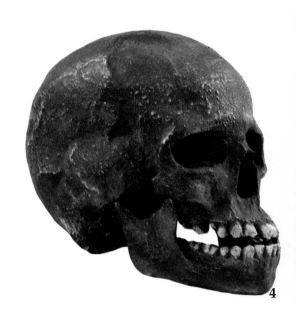

4

Homo sapiens

In previous pages we have seen how human species have gradually evolved. As forests in Africa were replaced by savannah, primate species survived by changing. When swinging through trees was no longer an advantage, hominoid species evolved a two-legged walk. They could walk and run better and they could use their hands to hold stones or sticks to defend themselves from faster runners. Some hominoids survived, not by being the fastest or the strongest, but by being the cleverest. They learned to use tools and to make tools. Neanderthals became experts at making beautifully formed stone tools. But it was with Homo sapiens that came creativity in tools, art and culture.

Cro-Magnons

The first modern humans to live in Europe are called Cro-Magnons. They were very different from the Neanderthals whom they replaced. We cannot tell from the fossils why the Cro-Magnons survived and the Neanderthals did not. Were the Cro-Magnons simply better adapted or was there a fight?

Certainly the Cro-Magnons seem to have been more creative. Using tools of bone, antler and ivory, as well as stone and wood, they were able to hunt all kinds of animals. They learned to fish and to catch birds. They even learned to preserve meat in permafrost. They had permanent or semi-permanent campsites with complex cooking hearths.

Attention to detail

The Cro-Magnon humans are also remarkable for their attention to fine details. They made clothing with bone needles. Carefully formed beads were used, sometimes by the thousand, to decorate their bodies. Cro-Magnons also decorated caves with beautifully painted images of animals and symbols. The symbols indicate that the paintings had more meaning than just decoration – they were linked with ceremonies or beliefs.

All of these activities required a complex means of communicating. Signs or grunts would not have been enough. Language and symbols would have been used, as they are today, to communicate between Homo sapiens.

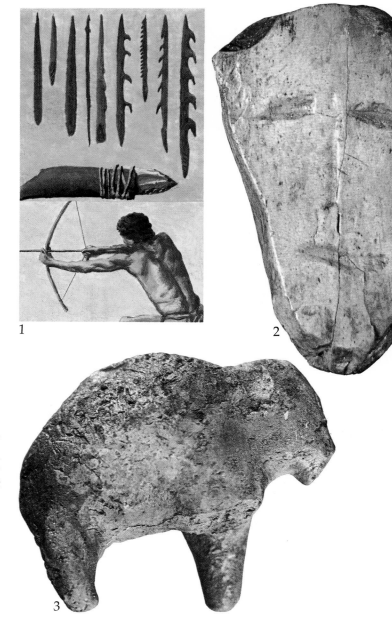

1

2

3

1 Homo sapiens created a range
of new tools. These included
harpoons made of reindeer bone,
stone tips attached to clubs or
spears, and bows and arrows.

2 Some Homo sapiens made
sculptures of stone, bone or clay.
This face, carved in ivory, was
found in Eastern Europe.

3 This mammoth, sculpted from
clay, also comes from Eastern
Europe.

4 This artist's impression shows
Homo sapiens in Africa. Their
permanent home is the mouth of a
cave. Animal skins give additional
shelter from cold and rain. In the
distance a camp in an open area
has huts covered with animal
skins. They have a wide range of
food from hunting and fishing.
Meats are treated and cooked.
Skins are carefully scraped and
dried and may be decorated.

5

5 These cave paintings seem to
tell a myth, or story. They
may have been part of a
religious ceremony.

6 These stone carvings in a
cave in Namibia show a
giraffe, a lion and other
animals.

6

1 *A statue found in Serbia shows a group of fisher-hunters and the myth about their origins.*
2 *This bone harpoon with barbs was found in a cave inhabited by Paleolithic hunters in the Czech Republic.*

Conclusions

Every human being is different. No one is the same as anyone else.

In different regions of the world there are variations in the colour of people's skin, the shape of their heads, in their hair, faces, eyes, noses and height.

Some differences have developed as a result of adaptation to the environment. For example, dark skin, which protects people from very penetrating rays of the sun, has evolved in the hottest regions of the world. In other regions, where the sun is less intense, skin is lighter in colour.

Despite the differences in physical appearance, we all share a common origin in our distant African ancestors. All human beings are able to think, plan and communicate by means of language. We are all able to enjoy beauty and to choose between right and wrong. We all belong to the same human family. We are different, but basically we are all the same.

Questions

In this book you have read about the stages in the development of human beings on Earth. Now you may want to think about these questions and the issues that they raise.

1 *Can we be really sure that things happened this way?*
Our knowledge of the evolution of humans is based on the evidence from fossils. But the way scientists interpret fossils and draw conclusions about them reflects their own thinking. In the future new discoveries may be made that support those conclusions or which change our present knowledge.

2 *Do humans come from apes?*
Based on the study of fossils, we can say that humans share a common ancestor with apes. That ancestor was very different from and was more developed than present-day apes. Human intelligence is demonstrated in the ability to reason, to plan and to enjoy beautiful things. It is this ability, this reaching out of the human spirit, which marks the difference between human beings and animals.

Glossary

adapt: to change over time to better suit the surroundings.

Australopithecus afarensis: a bipedal hominid that appeared about four million years ago. The skeleton Lucy is an example of this early ancestor.

Australopithecus africanus: a hominid that evolved from *Australopithecus afarensis.*

evolve: to change gradually over time.

extinct: a species that has died out is extinct.

fossils: the traces or remains of once-living things. Animal fossils might be bones, shells or even the trace of an animal, such as its footprint.

genus: a classification of living things that contains one or more related species. Modern humans are classified in the genus Homo (see page 28).

harpoon: a weapon that is thrown, similar to a spear. A point at one end pierced the animal, and hooks along the side held the harpoon in place. Harpoons could be attached to a stick and used for fishing (see page 41).

hominid: group of primates including humans, their fossil relatives, and great apes, such as chimpanzees, gorillas and orang-utans.

hominoid: group of primates including humans and apes, 'cousins of old-world monkeys'.

Homo erectus: human, lived from about one million to 300 000 years ago.

Homo ergaster: human, appeared over 1.5 million years ago. An ancestor of both *Homo erectus* and *Homo sapiens.*

Homo habilis: 'handy man'; human, lived from about 2 to 1.5 million years ago; shared many traits with Australopithecus.

Homo heidelbergensis: human, appeared about 500 000 years ago.

Homo neanderthalensis: human, appeared 200 000 years ago.

Homo sapiens: modern human, appeared about 100 000 years ago, only surviving member of the genus Homo.

Kenyapithecus: a hominoid that lived about 14 million years ago.

mammals: a group of warm-blooded vertebrates that have hair and suckle their young.

mammoth: an extinct relative of the elephant (see page 4).

primate: order of mammals that includes humans; evolved about 65 million years ago.

Proconsul: a hominoid that lived about 18 million years ago.

prosimian: a lower ape, includes bush babies, tarsiers, lemurs and many fossil primates.

Purgatorius: a primitive primate that lived about 65 million years ago.

species: a classification of a distinct group of living things that can mate and have offspring that can also reproduce. Over time a species can evolve into another species. Modern humans have evolved over time and are now classified as *Homo sapiens*, with *Homo* being the genus name and *sapiens* being the species name. Groups of related species, such as *Homo neanderthalensis* and *Homo sapiens*, belong to the same genus.

Index

Numbers in **bold** refer to illustrations.

EVOLUTION OF THE MONERAN, PROTIST, PLANT, AND FUNGI KINGDOMS

PLANT KINGDOM

MONERANS
PROTISTS*
FUNGI
BRYOPHYTES

PTERIDOPHYTES

GYMNOSPERMS

ANGIOSPERMS

Mosses

Licopods (club mosses)

Horsetails

Ferns

Cycads

Cordaites

Conifers

Ginkgo

Glossopteris

Cycadeoids

PSILOPHYTES
Zosterophyllum

PSILOPHYTES
Rhynia

Blue green bacteria

Bacteria**

*at least 1 billion years ago

**3½ billion years ago

CHLOROPHYTA
Green algae

Era	Period
Cenozoic	Holocene 0.01
	1.8 Pleistoc
	Pliocene
	Miocene
	Oligocene
	Eocene
	65 Paleocene
Precambrian	Cretaceo 140
	Jurassic 195
	Triassic 245
	Permian 280
	Carbonife 345
	Devonian 410
Mesozoic	Silurian 440
	Ordovicia 500
	Cambrian 570
Paleozoic	Precambri 700***

EVOLUTION OF THE PROTIST AND ANIMAL KINGDOMS

INVERTEBRATES

CHORDATES

VERTEBRATES

Sponges

Coelenterates

Segmented worms

Chelicerates

Crustaceans

Myriapods

Insects

Molluscs

Echinoderms

Hemichordates

Lancelets and Tunicates

Cartilaginous fish

Bony fish

Amphibians

Reptiles

Birds

Mammals

Trilobites

Jawless fish

***million years ago